A Story of the City:
poems occasional and otherwise

Ed Madden
Poet Laureate, City of Columbia, 2015-2022

A Story of the City:
poems occasional and otherwise

Ed Madden
Poet Laureate, City of Columbia, 2015-2022

A Story of the City:
poems occasional and otherwise

Copyright 2023 by Ed Madden. All Rights Reserved

Printed in the United States of America. No parts of this book may be reproduced in any manner without written permission except in the case of brief quotations embodied in critical articles and reviews.

Library of Congress Control Number: 2023942916
ISBN: 978-1-942081-34-0

Cover Photograph by Stephen Chesley
Cover Design by Lee Snelgrove

Contents

11	Foreword
15	Introduction

I

21	A story of the city
23	On a tour of the State House grounds
24	Stars
25	From the ashes
27	Walk back through the ashes
29	Hercules and the wagoner
31	Postcard: First Baptist Church, Columbia, SC
32	When we're told we'll never understand
34	The curse
35	Remember
37	Sweep
39	At the Gervais Street Bridge Dinner
40	The lesson that night
42	Postcard: Lincoln Street Tunnel
43	On a photograph of student protestors

II

46	The Gates
47	The sound of a needle on vinyl
51	Pollen
53	Translations
55	Nothing is perfect, everything is beautiful
57	At the corner of Lady and Main
61	Postcard: Main Street
62	Red, white, black, or before the eclipse

66   Something to declare

III

68   Which
69   Sherman sonata
78   A new year

IV

81   Body politic
84   Crossing
86   Postcard: Columbia Canal
87   survivor
89   Semi
90   Prayer
91   On considering the bronze bust of J. Marion Sims at the northwest corner of the South Carolina State House grounds
95   Window and wall, on Blue Sky's *Tunnelvision* (1975)
98   Better angels
101 Song
102 Not just a collar
105 Fireflies: Congaree National Park
106 A table big enough

V

110 When you look back, what do you see?
111 Two clocks on the same street
113 Then: pandemic postcards
116 At the Most Worshipful Prince Hall Grand Lodge
118 Crossing the borders
120 Aboard

121 Postcard: Boyd Greenhouse
122 Flag
123 Postcard: jimson weed

125 Notes
133 Thanks & Acknowledgments

Foreword

I remember the first time I sat at a table with Ed Madden.

Drue Barker, who was coming in as the new director of the women's studies program at USC, had come to town and Ed, Julia Elliott, and I had taken her down to the Hunter Gatherer pub on the university side of Main Street to chat.

It was sometime in 2007 and I felt like I was among royalty.

I knew of Julia because she sang in the alt-band Grey Egg, which may be the most innovative and eclectic musical group Columbia, SC has ever seen. She had copies of the band's most recent CD to share with Ed and Drue.

I knew of Ed because it seemed like everyone knew of Ed. A proudly-out gay man, his reputation as a poet and activist set a standard for community engagement. I'll admit now that these three people, all clearly commanders of their own fates, were a bit intimidating. I was just an adjunct instructor looking to find a new place to grow myself, having spent the last two decades teaching, writing, and watching my daughters grow into adults. If I had known then how many tables Ed and I would sit at together over the years to come, how many projects we would hatch and secrets we would share, I would have taken better note of our surroundings than I did. I would have recorded those observations like historical artifacts of the moment. I would have recognized that I was meeting a person who would play a unique and cherished role in the rest of my life.

Fast forward eight years and I had the proud pleasure of cheering Ed on as he took the title of Poet Laureate for the City of Columbia. A brave and selfless thing to do. Ed embraced the role like it was made for him, working with Lee Snelgrove to create a culture of renegade poetry at the same time that he seamlessly elevated the importance of poetry by creating beautiful and profoundly honest responses to the events that occurred in the life of the city.

As the first poet laureate in the capitol city of a state that has gone without a state poet laureate for three years and counting, Ed's position took on greater significance than it had to. While South Carolina's first state poet laureate, Archibald Rutledge, had served a lifetime appointment from 1934 until his death in 1973, followed in succession by Helen Von Kolnitz Hyer, Ennis Rees, Grace Freeman, and Bennie Sinclair, in 2020, Marjory Wentworth, the sixth person to hold the title, left the post and, as late as summer 2023, Governor Henry McMaster had failed to fill the position. In the absence of a government or appointing body following through on its responsibility to maintain the continuity of leadership in the poetic arts, poets throughout the state looked to Ed Madden as their guide. And guide them he did. Soon, city poets laureate were being named throughout the state in Charleston, Greenville, Rock Hill, the Pee Dee, and more.

Why does it mean so much to poets to be represented by an honored one of their own? Several reasons, none of which are monetary. In fact, the small budget once allocated to the state poet laureate was rescinded by former Governor Mark Sanford in 2000. There is a smaller budget for the Columbia city laureate, but it all goes toward supplies needed for various projects and never sees the inside of the laurcate's pocket.

It is validating to wordsmiths of all genres to have an artist among them who represents the importance of the part they play, we play, in the creation of our culture. The poet laureate of a city or state is a role model for all of us who confess our words and perceptions to paper in an attempt to make sense of the chaos that surrounds us. That person reminds us that the act of creative writing is not an exercise in frivolity but rather an important practice in interpreting the turns of events that make up our history.

Similarly, patrons of poetry depend upon the writers among us, especially our poet laureate, to help us find truth in ways that sooth and unite us. Time and again, Ed Madden reminded us that in addition to being a city of individuals whose unique gifts intimately design the world around us, we are also a cohort of creatures living life together at this particular place and time and are forever united by the community we create.

So much has changed over the almost two decades I've called Ed my colleague, friend, and collaborator. Neighbors have moved, both to and away from us. Elected officials have come to office, created policy, and moved on. Friends and allies have passed away from us, leaving their own legacies on the landscape of our home. And because Ed Madden used his inimitable gifts to record his perceptions of this community and commit them to paper to preserve for posterity, the record of our lives as citizens of Columbia, South Carolina will live on in the volume we hold in our hands—*A Story of the City: poems occasional and otherwise, Columbia, SC 2015-2022*.

Cynthia Boiter
Executive Director, The Jasper Project

Introduction

I had no understanding of the power of a city poet laureate. When Cindi Boiter approached me early in my time at One Columbia for Arts and Culture about creating a position of poet laureate for the city, I didn't know that those existed. But it seemed so logical. Why wouldn't we want someone that could bring gravity and reflection to events? Why not have another ambassador for Columbia's talented artists?

So, we created it. We worked to write a resolution and advocated to City Council for them to recognize the position. And Ed Madden rose to the top as the poet that could really set the tone for the position from the beginning. And that's exactly what he did in his two terms as Columbia's Poet Laureate.

Ed's work in the position has changed the way I and many other Columbians think about the role of poetry and words in our daily lives. He has brought together so many voices to think and write about what it's like to live in this city, what it means to be a Columbian, and why our culture is so important to us. He has utilized his platform to create joy, offer gravitas, express sorrow, confront grief, incite spontaneity, deepen introspection, tell stories, counter injustice, share history, and celebrate the art of language.

It has been a privilege to sit in the chair next to Ed and think about these projects, and in many cases help with the work of producing projects. I will forever have a divot in my finger from cutting so many cardboard letters for rain poetry stencils. I will never forget the exuberance of the day when volunteers distributed fake parking tickets across the city to fool people into reading a poem. I'll always hold dear the zine-style folded pamphlet we distributed with the poem "Better Angels."

Now, I can't imagine living in a city that doesn't recognize a poet laureate. It's so easy to empower someone to foster creativity. And it's necessary that city leaders utilize their power to recognize how culture is made and is cultivated.

Thank you, Ed, for making Columbia stronger and more vibrant. Thank you Columbia for stepping up and celebrating who we are and who we want to be.

Lee Snelgrove
Former Executive Director,
One Columbia for Arts and Culture

But where are we going to be, and why, and who?
The disenfranchised dead want to know.
We mean to be the people we meant to be,
to keep on going where we meant to go.

        Miller Williams, "Of History and Hope" (1999)

I

A story of the city

Written for the January 20, 2015 State of the City address by Mayor Stephen K. Benjamin.

In the story, there is a city, its streets
straight as a grid, and in the east, the hills,
in the west, a river. In the story,
someone prays to a god, though we don't
know yet if it is a prayer of praise
or a prayer for healing—so much depends
on this—his back to us, or hers, shoulders
bent. We hear the murmur of it, the urgency.

In the story a man is packing up
a box of things at a desk, a woman is sitting
in a car outside the grocery as if
she can't bring herself to go in, not yet.
Or is the man unpacking, setting a photo
of his family on the desk, claiming it?
And is the woman writing a message to someone—
her sister maybe, a friend? In the story,
a child is reading, sunlight coming through
the window. In the story, the trees are thicker,

and green. In the story, a child is reading,
yes, and his father watches, uncertain
about something. There is a mother, maybe
an aunt, an uncle, another father. These things
change each time we open the book, start
reading the story over. Sometimes a story
about trees, sometimes about a city
of light, the city beyond the windows of a dark
pub, now lucent and glimmering. Or sometimes
a story about a ghost, his clothes threaded
with fatigue and smoke, with burning—you smell him
as he enters the room, and you wonder
about that distant city he fled, soot-shod,

looking back in falling ash at the past.

Sometimes it's a story about someone
singing. Or someone signing a form, or speaking
before a crowd, or shouting outside a building
that looks important, if only for the flag there,
or the columns, or the well-kept lawn.
By now it's maybe your story, and the child
is your child, or you, or maybe we're telling
the story together, as people do, sitting
at a table in a warm room, the meal
finished, the night dark, a candle lit,
an empty cup left out for a prophet,
an empty chair, maybe, for a dead friend,
a room filled with words, filled with voices,
the living and the dead, someone telling
a story about the people we are meant to be.

On a tour of the State House grounds

at the Strom Thurmond Monument

No room at the top to list her,
the eldest sister, dropped in
at the bottom, an afterthought,
a smudge in the stone, a scar,

what no one would say or said
while he was alive, though now
he's dead, she's there, the lie
filled in, carved out again:

that four kids is five, and standing
ten-foot-tall is really
eight, that history is messy
and written too quickly, and what's

written in stone
is often wrong.

Stars

bullets in the dining room table and such

Never fixed, just six of them—
bronze stars affixed, bolted in,

a bronze for every occasion, cannon,

each mortar shell that picked a spot,
nicked the wall, its Winnsboro blue

(eleven shades of blue and grey)—

or knocked off a pediment, clipped
that windowsill that's still watching west,

botched up the façade with a bang,
a burn, a fist of rust that burnished

the stone, pockmarked, scarred,
permanent, done.

From the ashes

*Written for and read at the commemoration of the
Burning of Columbia, Boyd Plaza, February 19, 2015*

My granddad's house burned down when I was young.
I remember the family huddled around a table,
my uncle stunned, my aunt doing what she could,
and later going over to see the smolder

of what was left: a concrete pad beside
the road, smoke rising over the black
ashes, surrounded by morning and empty fields,
everything lost but for the clothes they wore.

A few years later, a tornado slammed a town
just south of us—a night my mother said
We need a storm cellar—we could hear it
at the house, the wind's angry whine.

We drove over the next morning to see
houses smashed, debris thrown across
the fields, clothing waving like surrender
in the stripped trees. Blackville was rebuilt

though never the same after, few people
left behind and houses left to rot,
left to bindweed and trumpet vine and rain.
My grandparents moved to a house in town.

~

That winter, back then, Columbia was a city
of cotton and wind, bags of cotton cut open
and carried into the trees. And the streets
looked as though covered in snow, a city

thick with cotton, waiting for Sherman.

That night the air was filled with sparks, pieces
of blazing shingles, *a perfect shower of fire,*
the effect of which was to light the whole city,

like something biblical, a city smitten with repentance.
The sparks were falling so thick, it was said,
the nuns fleeing the Ursuline Convent had holes
burned in their veils, burned in their black dresses.

Hundreds walked out from under burning roofs
into the cold and smoldering streets, and when
the sun came up, it was the next day.
And then the next day, and then the next.

Walk back through the ashes
an *ars poetica*

February 2015

In one story, an old black man
is the only one who died that night.

In another, soldiers trying to restore
discipline shot and killed two of their own.

In another, one told and retold to children,
there was a monster who burned down

the city, who would get you too
if you didn't straighten up.

At night, a woman ascends the capitol steps.
She carries the stories of the city

in her arms, tenderly, like a child,
like a dead boy, like a bolt of bright

cloth rescued from the flames.
Four figures scatter ashes down the street,

four or five dark figures and a child,
white sacks slung across their shoulders,

filled with the remains of old homes
burned down—grit of loss and burnt

offerings, the fictions we were taught,
bitterness Moses stirs into our tea.

History is salt, is cloth, is water, is ash.

~

There are gifts of whiskey in the story.

This is consistent, whether it is the story
of a day that begins with a mayor's

surrender amidst songs and celebration,
or the story of the night after,

a night of confusion and looting and smoke.
A woman twists in a skirt of flame.

Her face hidden, she can't see beyond
the cage of her dark and lovely bonnet.

Her skirt is a soldier's tent pitched
on the town green. Her skirt is

a marble statue of John C. Calhoun
in a Roman toga dissolving in a puddle

of quicklime and shame. Her skirt is a canvas
stretched across nine blocks. Her skirt

is historical drag, a stiff and difficult flag.
The new mayor will write a new letter.

A woman will lead us up the steps, sometimes
carrying the story of the city, sometimes

carrying a stone. Today her hands are empty.
Walk back through the ashes. Walk

back through the ashes. Walk back.

Hercules and the wagoner

June 2015, after the Charleston shooting

The hedgerow is filled with fireflies,
a ripple of light across the lawn,

signaling something or someone gone.
My father dies again this week.

He does it every year now.
My mother and brother at midweek prayer.

Tomorrow morning, we will hear the news.
Tonight, the heat does not break.

~

One loss grinds against another, greater.
One story writes over another, older.

History is a story of murder and things burning.
History is a story written in ashes.

Vesey's great revolt was to begin at midnight.
White folk burned his church to the ground.

Here is the church, here is the steeple.
Open the doors, here are the people.

~

Between prayers at the AME church
the day after, a senator

spoke to packed pews
about *the appalling silence of good people.*

Outside they all sang *this little light of mine.*

~

While playing Uno and Skip-Bo at the hotel,
Bert's family visiting for the weekend,

we try to talk about the rally we're missing.
A niece says, it's just a symbol. We stumble

again into these difficult conversations.
How do we make visible the privilege we breathe

like air? The cards fall by color and number.
Tiny, tired, my nephew leans against me,

his dark skin warm against mine.

~

Thunder rattled windows all over the city,
the rain falling finally, the heat finally

broken, right at the moment when—
as if we were in some melodramatic film—

the governor said the flag should come down.

~

Denmark Vesey's favorite fable was the tale
of Hercules and the Wagoner. A farmer's cart

slid into a ditch, got stuck in the mud,
a wheel sunk to its hub in a rut.

The farmer cursed his luck, said a prayer
to the hero Hercules, sure he'd lift it out.

Not so fast, a voice from heaven said.
Put your own shoulder to the wheel first.

Postcard: First Baptist Church, Columbia, S.C.

Justitia Virtutum Regina, motto of the City of Columbia

This is where they decided
to divide US, where they said
all men are not equal, where
they pledged allegiance to
the divided states of America
and to the secession for
which they stood, a nation
broken, divisible, with liberty
and justice for some.

When we're told we'll never understand

June 17, 2015, after the Charleston shooting

Someone says a drug-related incident,
someone says he was quiet, he mostly kept to himself,
someone says mental illness,
someone says *a hateful and deranged mind*,
someone says he was a loner, he wasn't bullied,
someone says his sister was getting married in four days,
a newsman says an attack on faith,
a relative says his mother *never raised him to be like this*,
a friend says *he had that kind of Southern pride, strong conservative beliefs*,
someone says *he made a lot of racist jokes, but you don't really take them seriously like that you don't really think of it like that*,
someone says he wanted to start a civil war,
he said he was there to kill black people,
the governor says *we'll never understand.*

~

He is not a lone wolf,
he is not alien,
he is not inexplicable,
he is not just *one sick individual*,
he is one of us,
he is from here,
he grew up here,
he went to school here,
he wore his jacket with its white supremacist patches here,
he told racist jokes here,
he got his gun here,
he learned his racism here,
his license plate sported a confederate flag here,
the confederate flag flies at the state capitol here,

he had *that kind of Southern pride,*

~

this is not isolated this is not a drug incident,
this is not unspeakable (we should speak),
this is not unthinkable (we should think),
this is not inexplicable (we must explain it),
he is not a symbol he is a symptom,
he is not a cipher he is a reminder,
his actions are beyond our imagining,
but his motivation is not beyond our understanding
no *he didn't get those ideas from nowhere.*

mental illness is a way to not say *racism*
drug-related is a way to not say *hate*
loner is a way to not say *one of us*
we'll never understand is a way to not say *look at our history*

Look away, look away, look away [to be sung]

The curse

after Genesis 9:20-29

"*God did this, and it is in his holy word.*"
> letter to The State *newspaper, 22 August 2017, using Genesis 9 to argue that God created slavery*

We heard it growing up, a story about
a boat, a rainbow, and Noah getting drunk,
Old Testament riddle rendered racist fable.
A father curses his son to be a servant
of servants, even among his brothers, now other
to them—Ham, a man whose name they used
to say meant *burnt* though it doesn't. A man
who'd never learned a foreign tongue cites Hebrew
to instruct us on the way it was (or is) meant
to be, bully pulpit bigot exegesis for brothers
willing to walk backwards, to look the other
way to not see that it's not a story about
fathers or honor or enslavement but the shame
of what we do, what we have done to one another.

Remember

that summer the yellow spiders
invaded, gold bangles dangling
in the dark green trees—
webs glowing gold at sunset?
The year of all the funerals.
Then the storms came, the rains,
golden webs swept away,
the red spider lilies lifting
from the soaked lawn, ready
to guide the dead home.

Sweep

after the historic floods, October 2015

The sun was nothing and then was gone,
a scrim of rain pulled across the lawn.

~

Later, something woke us in the dark—
downstairs, below the wind's wet snarl,

water coming through the wall,

steady seep and runnel, rising slow.
How long, how fast, we couldn't know—

brown water pooling at the step,
water surging over and under the road.

~

We took a broom, at first, swept it out—
the brown water pooling at the step—

across the sweep-seal, weather-stripped,
the useless weep holes in the threshold—

what we could do, though it was not,
though it was never

enough
to hold off

the batter

of wind and water—
never

enough
to hold it off.

~

The horses of the dark, they never stop,
water surging over and under the road.

They never stop, the horses of the dark.

~

The wind a whip, the storm drummed the roof,
pummel of insistent hooves,

water moving through basement walls,
water surging over and under the roads,

over and under the useless bridges,
over and under the useless streets—

pavements caved and carved away
beneath the brown swell's dirty sweep

and over and over on tv
that title loan shop,

its small awning and crumpled walls
leveled in one great slow wave.

~

After it all, the sodden drift and spill of things,
rotten whiff of heaped debris,

abandoned homes on altered streets,
survivors sifting through what remained,

the difficult work of cleaning up,
the relentless work of going on.

At the Gervais Street Bridge Dinner

Written after the first bridge dinner, October 18, 2015, and later read for Mayor Stephen K. Benjamin's State of the City address, January 26, 2016.

And here we all are, this golden hour
on the river, on a bridge between

two cities, a bowl of blue sky
and gold light above us, the brown water

below us, behind us, beyond,
the current beneath all our conversations,

and later the lanterns all coming on.

~

J. says there was this woman, Rachel,
not really affected, but needed to do

something, needed to help—there, in his
neighborhood, clipboard in hand, she made

sure that everyone got what they needed
as the floods receded down the streets,

and people assessed what was left.

~

Someone makes a toast—to the first
responders walking by, a downed policeman,

to people making their way together, finding
their feet, together. A mayor says the rivers

don't divide us, they bring us together,
and with each toast we make—all of us

gathered at the long tables, the river
threading our conversations—with each toast

a gust of wings above us, a flyover of geese
following the river home, and in the dark,

the rough voices still singing.

The lesson that night

June 17, 2016, a year later

"And these are they likewise which are sown on stony ground."
  Mark 4:16

"Who are we now?"
  Nikky Finney, "A New Day Dawns"

How hot it was that sun-beat week,
watering the yard every day,
the curled leaves and dry ground,
green wings of zinnia breaking the soil.
They sat together around a green table,
prayed, sang, then opened the gospel—
the lesson that night was seed sown
on stony ground. What can we know
of the human heart, entangled in all
that we've been taught? A boy from here
sat with them about an hour,
then aimed his hate and opened fire.

~

How quick we were to act,
focused on that festering flag,
quick to take it down
and move forward, move on—
these aren't the same.
After weeks of heat, it rained the day
the governor said to take it down.
Are we somehow different now?
How would we know?

~

We furled a flag. We furled a flag.
A girl was slung across a room,
a man who ran shot in the back.
The broke and broken schools remain.
What has changed, beyond that square
of empty sky where it once flew,
the opened door of clouds and blue?

~

The lesson that night was stony ground.
Not birds, not thorns, not the good soil.
What grows up quick among the stones.
What has no roots, what withers away.
A friend calls change a perennial plant.
A second year takes nurture and luck.
If it comes back another year,
a better chance that it will stay.

Water well the just-sown and just-up.
Water long in morning light.
Water long and soak the roots
to learn the lesson of that night.
        Learn the lesson of that night.

Postcard: Lincoln Street Tunnel

Words appear like light
and shadow on the floor.

Nothing above, no source,
the walls are lined with night.

What counts for wisdom in
the dark? That scrap of sky

that leads us out.

On a photograph of student protestors

> *after a photograph of students from Benedict College and Allen University protesting segregation on Columbia's Main Street, March 2-3, 1960*

In the picture from 1960 Columbia,
students all dressed smart and walking
up Main Street from the south and east,

one young man up front is just stepping
into the street with his books slung loose
against his hip, his tie a black exclamation

against his white shirt, and a white woman
in a dark fur standing beneath McCrory's
gray awning holds her bag of goods

against her like a child, huddles beside
a line of men who seem to block the doors.
She watches the young men and young women

walking by, carrying books as if they had
just left class to make their way downtown,
or as if, maybe, they thought they might study

a bit, sitting at the counter, or as if
they would just go back to class, once
this necessary errand was done. They don't

look at her or at the men. They look
straight ahead, into the future.

The Gates

November 9, 2016, after the election

Bert's up early, bringing in the boxes
from last night's auction, detritus of someone's life.
He shows me a painting, a street scene somewhere
in Philadelphia, warm with autumn light.
The table lot went cheap, all art, framed things.
The yard rustles with leaves, the trees shaking
their lives off in the dark—what they've been doing
all week, roots sunk deep for what's to come.
The woman who bid against him told him she just
wanted the frames. That some of them were filled
with sketches, photos of Christo's ephemeral work,
only made his story more beautiful this morning
as he told it, as he unloaded the truck, the walk
brittle and ankle-deep in dead leaves.

The sound of a needle on vinyl

> *Based on responses to a question posted on social media about first experiences with arts and culture, this poem was written/compiled for the launch of Amplify, a comprehensive cultural plan for the Columbia area, Township Auditorium, January 29, 2018.*

I give you the macramé owl, the one with broken pinecones for eyes.

I give you the candy dish on the coffee table, its hard nuggets of sugar and color stuck together.

I give you the turkey made from a drawing of your hand.

I give you those big picture books with cracked spines that your mother read to you, the way her voice changed to shape the story.

And then there's your dad, putting on the Rolling Stones' *Exile on Main Street*, turning it up and dancing around. Not gracefully, a little unhinged, but with a lot of passion.

I give you that first concert—was it Michael Jackson? You memorized the names of all five Jacksons, memorized the songs. You were jealous of your cousin's pierced ear, that dangling glove earring. You slept with his albums under your bed in hopes that you would dream of him and his tiger. You were eight.

Can you see the little girl in pigtails, dancing in the dining room till dinnertime?

Or the little boy obsessed with mime?

I give you that moment someone explained to you that when someone dies onstage it's make-believe.

I give you that moment you fell asleep during the musical, or during church, and then when you woke up during the last song, you thought you had woken up in heaven.

What was the first song that made you cry?

Do you remember the first time you smelled a darkroom?

I give you the bright plaster tropical fish swimming across Aunt Betty's bathroom, fish not found in nature, but found in Aunt Betty's bathroom.

I give you the bronze and copper statues of deer in your grandfather's office, the way they felt in your hand when you played with them. You were not supposed to play with them. The doe with a relief image of a fawn on her stomach.

I give you the stiletto heels you mother spray-painted gold and placed elves inside, your favorite Christmas decoration.

Who was the child in that framed portrait at the back of Granny Lola's house? Was the child dead? They used to do that. I give you that dark, hand-carved frame.

I give you the old man at your grandma's church who taught you to sing with shaped notes. It was serious business. It was like a foreign language.

I give you the women's syncopated clapping, the shuffling of feet, the bending and rising of bodies with the lyrics of the song.

I give you that moment you picked out your mom among the other women, sure you heard her voice alone.

I give you Mrs. Slavin's weekly music class, the five-line chalk holder she used to draw a musical staff on the board, the way it would sometimes squeal, then she'd write in the notes. You loved her weekly visits and the songs she taught you. You still remember "Hava Nagilah."

I give you Leontyne Price and some guy singing on PBS when you were flipping through the channels. It was *Samson and Delilah*. You didn't understand what they were saying, but you were, for that moment, in another world.

I give you the first time you saw deaf people waving their hands in applause. It was after a dance performance. Their silence and motion were as beautiful as the dance.

Do you remember the May Day celebration at Earlewood Park, decades ago, your dress made of crepe paper—it was the prettiest dress in the world—crepe paper like the streamers, weaving in and out, plaiting the pole.

I give you your mother laying out the pattern for a dress on the dining table and cutting out the fabric pieces.

I give you Spirograph, Etch-a-Sketch, string art, Light Bright, Play-doh, and that little plastic potholder loom.

I give you the oriental rug in the floor of your family's military housing. It mesmerized you. You could ride the elephants all day.

I give you the black and white prints of classical architecture—Ionic, Doric, acanthus leaves—hanging in the cramped rooms of a tract home.

Your aunts would tell stories in the living room, and your uncles would tell stories outside under the oak trees. When did you realize that these were very different stories?

I give you your uncle's swanky Eames chair.

I give you the drum solo in "In-A-Gadda-Da-Vida" by Iron Butterfly. You listened to it with your dad in the car. It's the reason you took drum lessons.

I give you your mother singing, her clear powerful soprano, until chemotherapy and radiation took her voice away.

I give you the organ in the corner no one ever played.

Your father brought it home from the war, that little Swiss-made wooden music box. Your mother used to wind it up and place it on your pillow when you lay down for a nap. When your father died, your mother gave it to you.

When was it you realized you were tone-deaf and started to sing only in the car or in your head? I want you to sing again.

I give you Aunt Mary's sound system, the red velvet panels and wood carvings, and the sound of Billie Holiday.

I give you Billie Holiday's voice and the crackling sound of a needle on vinyl.

I give you the crackling sound of a needle on vinyl.

Pollen

on Andy Warhol's Jimmy Carter 1, *Columbia Museum of Art*

His hand is a fist but it is not a fist. His watch is on the inside of his wrist. Doctors do that, and nurses. So do farmers. It's so you don't scratch the crystal when you're doing manual labor, doing something difficult. Is this a signal? He is about to do something difficult.

He is like some superhero with those big blocks of color, that serious face. But it's not the red, white, and usual blue, but red, white, and—peach, and yellow. An image that feels weirdly resonant, charged with ambivalence. There is a flag, maybe, behind him, but in his hand a yellow book.

What blocks of color do we use to print out what we remember?

It's 1976, and I'm wearing my Bicentennial bellbottom jeans, with their red, white, and blue stitching on the back pockets. I think they were hand-me-downs from my youngest uncle. I was 12 years old.

We were excited when Jimmy Carter first ran. He was Southern, a farmer, like my dad and my uncles.

But then came Midge Costanza and my mother's stint in STOP ERA. I remember my parents' anger at Jimmy Carter. And those tractorcades in 1978 and 1979 that went to DC to protest. We had a tractor in those protests, drove all the way from Arkansas to the Mall.

I don't remember if my parents voted for him the first time, in 1976, though I'm sure they didn't when he ran against Ronald Reagan in 1980.

A farmer, did he betray farmers? A Southerner, did he leave the South?

His watch is on the inside of his wrist. He is about to do something very hard.

What does it mean to leave what you love? What does it mean to betray?

His hand is a fist but it is not a fist.

He holds a book the color of pollen.

Translations

Originally written for Transgender Memorial Day service at Washington Street United Methodist Church, November 20, 2015, this poem was later revised and read for the Lavender Graduation Ceremony at the University of South Carolina, December 1, 2015.

In writing class today, the students choose colors from a deck of discarded paint cards from the home supply store—names as plain as pencil point, as rich as sacred soil. I tell them to write a poem in which they make a home of the color. One student imagines a house of *drizzle*, another a home of *quaking grass*. There's driftwood and cardboard and recycled glass, the inbetween of *tadpole green*—everyone has their own color—a pale white called *hush*, like a page on which nothing is written yet, and there's *daybreak* and *gateway gray*, *potter's clay*, everyone their own color, their own home.

My Irish teacher explains to us that in Irish a black man is a blue man, *an fear gorm*, because the Irish for black man, *an fear dubh*, means the devil. The sky tonight is dark blue, it gets darker and darker. A light shines in the dark street like a sign, a kind of hush. I think about the way we use light and dark, white and black, to mean good and evil, as if this is just the way it is and not a set of boxes we put things in.

Maddy asks what her color means. She has chosen a color of plum, color of bruise—*framboise*, it says, meaning raspberry. A poem starts to knock about in my head, an incantation, almost, of sound—*framboise*, flamboyant, boys, laws, *because*.

My nephew and niece held a party this fall, what they called a reveal. It was raining, the sky was gateway gray and drizzle. There were pink and blue things everywhere, a special cake, a box of pink and sparkly socks, and across the table, ninja turtles. The baby is assigned a box before it's here, the way we do, before they're even born.

My Irish teacher says that unlike other languages, Irish has no neutral gender, so all nouns and pronouns are either masculine or feminine, but the Irish word for girl, *cailín*, is a masculine noun.

Caleb says, one way of thinking is that some people are red, and others are blue, and everyone understands this, but sometimes we come across someone who is purple. Purple, Caleb says, can be perceived as a mix of red and blue, but it's really a color on its own. A color like *framboise*, or daybreak, or hush.

David chooses *lotus*, his card a pale pink. I describe the lotus flower, its links with rebirth and awakening, the way that it emerges from the pond's muck, breaks the surface, transcends the mud and water to flower, awaken, become what it must become, something beautiful. Buddhists say it means that we can rise above our human suffering, move from one state to another. But maybe we can't really rise above our suffering, though we might try to ignore or forget.

The sky tonight is pencil point. Our skin is potter's clay. In Japan, there are lotus viewing parties, *so many flowers achieve enlightenment at the same moment, it is said, you can hear the blooms as they crack open.* In the Victorian language of flowers, *lotus* meant *forgetfulness*, or sometimes now *eloquence*, as if there might be some connection between the two. I think of a candle, a hush, a page with no words yet. I think of a pond filled with blossoms, a crowd of people holding candles at a vigil. I think of a room filled with students, moving on, lifting themselves, lifting us.

Nothing is perfect, everything is beautiful

an elegy for Leslie Pierce, July 25, 2015

What strikes me, when I look at his face—
José Ribera's lanky Saint Sebastian—
is the look of exasperation, impatience.
He looks up at the sky, not at all
like all those figures of religious ecstasy
and pain, but as if to say *what now,
God, what's next?* As if to say, the sky
here is beautiful, but nothing's perfect,
and I'm tired of this, really tired.
This Sebastian is tired, and he is beautiful,
one hand still hooked in rope, tied
above his head, the other loose, held
out, open—an offering, a gesture:

everything is beautiful, nothing is perfect.

On my desk I keep this small work
left over from that fall project with Leslie,
one of her collages, Ribera's Sebastian
leaning back on an ad for cameras
clipped from an old French magazine—
one of those things Leslie would find
and think useful, beautiful. Sebastian raises
his eyes to the cursive headline written
in the sky above him: *Ne perdez pas
votre temps!* Don't waste your time.
Nothing's perfect, but anything can be art,
Leslie's expansive aesthetic, something found
and kept, a scrap of print saved, remade:

nothing's perfect, anything is beautiful.

The cameras and their beautiful names circle him,
surround him—*exacta*, retina, ikon, *lumière*,
these machines of light and memory, black
boxes that stay time, hold the moments
we don't want to lose. That time
Leslie got tickled as we talked about
Ribera's *Immaculate Conception*—same
artist as the Sebastian—and she pointed out
the hands you barely see, the Virgin first
painted with hands crossed on her breast,
reverent, ready for a blessing, but then
painted over, hands clasped in prayer,
the old hands still there, like ghosts—

like the past not lost, still there, beautiful.

I can still hear her laugh, a chuckle
like a clear ripple in the air, the dove
descending on Mary. I wish that I had told her
that Mary's ghost hands are making the sign
for bear in sign language—she would've
loved that, the irreverent juxtaposition
like her own collages, and our laughter
echoing down the gallery. For our show,
Leslie took Alejandro's austere Sebastian,
a brute in a blizzard of arrows, and Hello-
Kitty-fied the prints with gaudy color—
gloriously irreverent, the pain edged
with humor and glitter, relentless, pretty, a life.

Nothing's perfect, everything is beautiful.

At the corner of Lady and Main

South Carolina Pride, September 3, 2016

Here at the corner of Lady and Main,
I'm thinking about a First Lady—
not the former First Lady who may
become the first, but the first
First Lady, the one this street's named for,
her husband, Washington, a block away.
And I'm thinking about Kenny Rogers,
or maybe Lionel Richey, who wrote
the song—*Lady, for so many years
I thought I'd never find you*—and after
so many years of marching around
this city and state, we found the place,
Lady and Main, and we're here, we're queer,
and we're ready, I think, for a party.

Here at the corner of Lady and Main
I'm thinking about where and when
we live. Ten years ago and a block
behind me, a bunch of men decided
to put an amendment on the ballot
for that November, and they would fight
to the bitterest end to keep our love
illegal. That March, a group of students
stuck black tape across their mouths
in a room of legislators who liked
to talk about us but not to listen.
Ten years ago this very week,
a rich white guy complained when our
campaign included anti-racist
training. He said that he would cancel
his fundraiser and cut off his donations
to the cause, if we made race
a part of what we do. We did,
we worked hard, and lost the vote,

but still we won, and still the work's not done.

Here at the corner of Lady and Main,
I'm humming Lionel Richie, but maybe
also a little Lady Marmalade,
since I'm sure there are some
voulez-vous couchez avec moi
conversations out there in the street,
as there should be on a gorgeous day like today.

Here at the corner of Lady and Main,
Main is straight, stops at the statehouse.
There's a wig shop or two, a few
places to eat, and the only theatre
in town that shows that queer film
you really wanted to see, and Main
may lean and swerve around as you head
up north and out of town, but here
it's a street that's very straight
that begins and ends at the state.
Stand here at the corner of Lady
and Main and you can't help but think
about gender and race, whose story
gets told, whose stories don't, here
on a street that stops at a monument
to men who died fighting for a lie
they'd been told, that black bodies
only matter when they're bought and sold.

Here at the corner of Lady and Main,
I'm thinking it's nice that Lady runs
athwart, across, she runs at odds
to Main, reminds us there are other
places to go, other ways to live
than those dictated a block away.
She lingers by the river, heads over
to Waverly, the city's first suburb,
a home to black artists and activists.

Lady reminds us of place and time,
one end rooted in a history of civil
rights, the other ending at the river
that keeps sweeping by, gone
before you can hold it in your hand.
She keeps a little distance between
herself and that big copper dome
that kept out blacks too long, doesn't
welcome many women, and has never
seen an open queer of any gender
or color take a seat at the table.

Here at the corner of Lady and Main,
I remember when I was growing up,
in church, we talked about the kingdom,
about living in this world but living
for another at the same time.
It's like living in two worlds at once.
A few years ago at Charlotte Pride,
there at the corner of Tryon and Trade,
three people in a row stopped by
the South Carolina table to say
that they were the only gay in Gaffney.
They had to go to Charlotte to be free.
There were at least three queers in Gaffney
who didn't know each other, couldn't
see each other. They had to go
somewhere else to see what was possible.

So here at the corner of Lady and Main,
look around, and see what's possible.
Live what is possible, love
who you want to love, and be kind
to one another. Sometimes we're not
that kind to one another. There is no
somewhere over a rainbow, somewhere
a place for us. This is the place.

Put the rainbow here at the corner
of Lady and Main, and make of the here
and now a future—a *there* and *then*, not *if* but *when*.

Postcard: Main Street

at the intersection of Gervais and Main

Look at the statehouse now
from the south.

Notice a bank logo
hangs beside the dome—

banks looking over
the legislature's shoulder.

Red, white, black, or before the eclipse

Bali / Charlottesville VA, Aug 14, 2017

The darkness drops again – W. B. Yeats

Odd to see it there in the old temple this summer, the sign
of wellbeing—a bent cross turning, a swastika, the sun—
so odd to see it in stone, even though we know it means

it meant something different. Was that the same temple
   where they
said Hindu and Buddhist pilgrims prayed together, bathed
together in holy water, until they no longer did? The place

was holy; we wore the red sarongs required to enter.
That seems so long ago. Back home we see flags the color
of blood, that bent cross, stark, in black and white. At Tirta

Empul's holy springs we didn't bathe, despite an offer
of lockers and green robes. Bert said it felt wrong
to step into someone else's sacred ritual. We watched

wet tourists standing waist-deep in the pool smile
for selfies, flash peace signs. It didn't feel holy. Still,
there among grinning tourists and Hindu faithful, we'd
   filled

a water bottle, not knowing what for. Tanah Lot
felt different, the sky white with rain, the sun a bright spot
out on the face of the sea. Our guide said our offerings

would help with renovations, so we fell in line, leaned over
the pool to wash our faces. Priests daubed foreheads with
   water
and rice, tucked frangipani behind our ears, the tide

coming in
the beach a babble
of scattered voices,

a book
of useless phrases
in my pocket.

~

The Balinese wrap trees and statues in sarongs of checkered
    black
and white like men at worship, the harmony important,
    balance.
Guardian figures flank a temple door. Our guide explained
    a mace

against the left shoulder means evil, mace against the right,
good. Otherwise they look the same. You must have both,
he said, but you have to see the difference. Everywhere

we saw small offerings at doorsteps, bright flowers and rice
cupped in leaves woven with prayer. The air was incense
    and kites,
everywhere the empty black chair of the god of gods, outside

every home, in every field, at the bend of every road,
at the bookshop where we bought incense blessed
by a priest and bound together with braided thread, red,

white, and black. Temple signs still forbid entrance
to menstruating women. A woman at the coffee market
asked why travelers don't like Trump. We talked difference

and fear. *You are you*, she pointed at Bert. *I am me.*
We accept. The only lingams we found were gaudy
bottle-openers in souvenir stalls. Our last day in Bali,

| 63

we found a small bird shuddering on our front step—
small sounds and then it was still. Bert scooped it up
gently, left it in the flowers. It felt something like a sign.

One day, when I told Wayan I'm a teacher, he pulled over
for a large statue of Saraswati, so I could see her better,
her book and lute, her beads, her swan, her jar of water.

One night, as he drove us back, we saw men in white
shirts and dark sarongs walking along the road, the night
quiet. Wayan drove slow. *They're going to temple*, he said,

The thin line of men and boys, torches lifted, thickened
into a crowded procession, women with baskets, children,
and then at the end, like a grinning apparition

from the dark, the barong—more giant dog than lion,
more muppet than rough beast, great shaggy guardian
of the good, and then it was gone,

and we drove on,
and darkness
dropped

again,
took back
the road.

~

Coming back, jet lag was hard, our bodies on a different
   clock,
the news one long banner of anger, hard to watch,
men in white shirts lifting torches on a college lawn,

and then the air was tear gas and mace, banners
wielded as weapons, that old sun sign back on flags
and armbands the way we know it now, in white and black.

A card tucked with the incense said to wear the braided
thread around the right wrist for protection, red,
white, and black. I've placed Saraswati on my desk,

the bracelet on my wrist. Soon, a wave of darkness will pass
over us, the sun gone, the air cold. We'll wear the glasses
that let us look into the dark without going blind. Our last

day there in Bali, we avoided news from home.
We ate breakfast at a French bakery, watched a woman
bless the ATMs across the parking lot. At the museum,

we picked our favorites. Bert stood at the fountain
of Ida Sang Hyang Widhi Waça, radiant and one,
god of all gods, beams of light like spikes shining from

his body, like forks at each joint, his genitals a curling
trident of light. For me it was the painting of Rahu swallow-
    ing
the sun, light shining between his teeth, the sun emerging

from his severed throat. Everywhere,
that last day there, I remembered,
tried to remember

to say thank you
in their tongue—
suksuma.

That evening,
when we returned
to our rooms,

Bert washed the step
with the bottle
of holy water.

Something to declare

July 11, 2018, after William Stafford

The president is overseas this week, that's the news,
and we're reading William Stafford in a chilly classroom
and trying to write about where we live now, and how.

Important people are gathered around a big table,
but we sit at our little desks. Sachi talks about what it means
to declare something when you cross a border.

Back home, I know my cat is dying. She'll amble
stiffly to the door when I return, her blind eyes
wide and bright with what she cannot see.

They say that history is going on somewhere.
Zoe describes her story as a scrap of paper swept
by the wind, litter snagged in a tree.

This is only a little report from a summer arts camp,
where Makenna and Maya and Eva and Micah are writing
about their small, rich lives. We're here. You can find us
    here.

Which

Ahead, the day that burns my face.
Behind, the day that darkens my back.
Which is the future, which the past?

Sherman sonata

> *I write hastily, as hastily as I think and speak, and I know full well that I often write and speak things that should have remained unsaid. – General W. T. Sherman*

1. 8 October 2014, after the Supreme Court let the appeals court ruling stand / ***andante***

Tonight, the streetlights shine the same, but some
other light limns the trees and lights
the street, glosses the lawn, the drive a glimmer

of not quite, not yet, as if the air
were filled with sparks, *the air filled with sparks
and small pieces of blazing shingles, the effect*

of which was to light the entire city....
but no, not yet, not now.
My bright-eyed redheaded fellow signed

a form, his grin the only hint that this
was just beginning. He's off at an auction
tonight, sorting through the debris of history,

and I'm trying to write about what happened.
It's the interval, the world tilts and things
rumble across the dark stage, the angels

flee the burning city, and surely Sherman
is headed this way, tonight, burning
bits of furniture and insurrection.

~

My mother doesn't answer my call. Maybe
she's heard the news, maybe she's afraid
of what I might say. Another night

she said she gets so disheartened by what's
happening in this country, that it reminds her
of my lifestyle, by which she means that man

she's never met, though I've lived with him
for twenty years. Her porch is stacked with wood,
the cold months ahead. I'll call again

another night. Beyond the window, the dark
city, the streetlights shining, an auction, an army,
a redheaded man sifting history, again.

~

The end of the world, someone said.
Or maybe this: the world moves on.

A judge, a decision, a form, a fee;
a groom signed where a bride could be.

A blaze of light in every word.
It doesn't matter which you heard.

The air is filled with fire and light.
The air is filled with fire and light,

2. Under the flag / *adagio*

A soldier smuggles a vase he stole from someone's home—
ceramic, silver, plunder.

Contrabands, a name for escaped slaves behind Union lines.

Slave marriages had no legal standing.

~

Sodom. Sherman. Columbia burning—

these burning cities thread a meditation on the night after
  we heard
what the court had done,

or not done,
and the whole fucking world changed

or not, not yet anyway,
because we didn't know yet what we could do.

What we would do.

~

It was not until after slavery was abolished
that marriage could be secured as a civil right.

Despite resistance from erstwhile Confederates,
Congress passed the Civil Rights Act of 1866,

which extended the right to make contracts,
including the right to marry, to all former slaves.

~

These juxtapositions are risky, I know that—

Sherman, Bert. Marriage,
those resistant Confederates.

Fugitive slaves would appeal to military officers
to marry them under the flag.

Sherman wrote a friend, *A n***** as such
is a most excellent fellow, but he is not fit to marry,*

to associate, or to vote with me and mine.

~

I got a nice vase which I will try to get home—
a soldier wrote, adding, *(It's broke now).*

~

We didn't know yet what we could do, or when.

3. What They Said / *scherzo*

That he was tall and lank.
That his nose was bladelike.
That his eyes were small and bright.

That he was a bright-eyed, red-headed fellow,
who was always prepared for a lark of any kind.
That he was incapable of dissembling,

and often blurted out the truth
as he accepted it in a way that was not acceptable
to his hearers.

That his presence, the impact of him, was very striking.
That he was outsized, standing nearly six feet.
That he wore a size nine shoe.

    That he would spare the libraries.

That his physique was narrow and almost effeminate.
That the pronounced crow's feet at the corners of his eyes
would gradually spread across his cheeks.

That his rusty beard was trimmed close.
That his hair was a thatch he rubbed up with his hands.
That he had coarse red hands.

That there was a certain carelessness about his clothing.
That at best his attitude toward such things seemed to be
   one of indifference
and on campaign it descended to plain negligence.

That he would wear his coat flapping open
and his vest buttoned only at the bottom.
That his uniform was often wrinkled and soiled.

That the streets were covered
with wind-blown cotton as if covered with snow.

That photographs show slender hands with long tapering
   fingers.
That there was a restlessness about him.
That he was fitful and agitated.

That he had a vigorous distinctive gait,
that he jerked himself along.
That when he listened to music,

his eyes danced in every direction and on everything.
That his fingers would nervously twitch his whiskers, coat
   buttons,
play a tattoo on his table or chair, or run through his hair.

That one moment his legs were crossed, the next both feet
   were on the floor.
That he would sit for a moment, then pace the floor.
That he was never quiet.

   That the air was filled with sparks and small pieces of
      blazing shingles.

That he was cocksure, mercurial, flighty, manic.
That when excited, his speech was rapid-fire.
That his mind was a splendid piece of machinery

with all of the screws a little loose.
That he could not reason—
that is, his mind leaped quick from idea to idea.

That he reached conclusions, they said, the way women did,
   instantly and intuitively.
That he was given to extravagance of expression,
a tendency to exaggerate.

That he too often said what he thought, that he was frank.
that his vigorous language and free use of tongue could get
   him into trouble.
That to admit error was harder for him than most men,

and that he did so very rarely.
That he kept irregular hours.
That he read political news voraciously,

that he was addicted to the very newspapers he would
   denounce.
That he took delight in maps, and had a flawless memory of
   topography,
that he never forgot a house, a road, a bayou.

That bourbon was his preference, but he never became
   drunk,
though he did become very mellow.
That he was a member of no church, but leaned toward
   Deism.

    That he was a barbarian, a vandal, a monster.

That he was a good, kind man.
That his friends called him *Cump*.
That he was unrelenting

in walking the path marked out for himself.
That this stern and relentless master of war
had *a heart as gentle and tender as a woman's.*

That the utter silence after it all was so startling
that when a wild bird sang you looked around, surprised.

IV. 20 November 2014 / *andante*

So here we are, back where we started,
a courtroom, a form, the world not ending.

The legal stay lifted like a cloud,
like a bar across a heavy door.

We dropped by the day before, paid
the fee, made our plans, went home as we had

for twenty years, wondering what the morrow
would bring. *The day is extremely beautiful, clear*

sunlight, Sherman wrote, *with bracing air*
and an unusual feeling of exhilaration

seems to pervade all minds. By then
he was grizzled and driven, his uniform surely

shabbier than usual, no longer the angelic ginger
man we saw in the national gallery in DC,

who in some uncanny way reminded me
of Bert. I sign my name in the wrong place,

at first, have to scratch it out and sign it
right, beneath the blue scribble. Something

to think about, signing outside the box,
but Bert signs the box marked *Bride,*

and still it's legal, signed by both, and witnessed
by a friend, the judge our officiant

that very bright and very cold morning.
I gave up on writing a love poem

to Cump, instead I write one to Bert:
I sign my name. I imagine walking out

of the flames, a bird in a cage in one hand,
his hand in the other, we walk out

from the burning city into the cold
air, and hundreds, nay thousands with us,

walking with us, the air filled with fire
and light. The air is filled with fire and light.

A new year

Bert's outside taking down the strings
of lights, this winter sun bright enough
for a new day, new year. Colleen sent
a thick heart made of seeds—we'll hang it
in a tree today for birds, for the winter
that persists despite the sun. Last night's
fireworks were gorgeous, though Barry ran back
and forth with his torch to relight them—
the way, sometimes, we have to do for
our little resolutions, for our glorious
dreams, for our tired hearts, when it's
dark, when it's still so cold.

IV

Body politic

Written for the January 31, 2017 State of the City address by Mayor Benjamin.

Even so the body is not made up of one part but of many.
I Corinthians 12:15

When thousands of women with pink hats
and placards fill the streets, think
about how a city handles
bodies, guides them down sidewalks
and streets, between walls of stone
and state, about the way a mass
of bodies is a way of saying
something, as when a march exceeds
its brief circuit of the city
and ends up on the interstate,
as if to say these bodies matter,
precarious, here and now. A city
is a body, the old philosophers
say, a leader the head, the soldiers
his hands. A church, they say, or palace
is like a brain, a place to pause,
reflect. Or it's the heart, stained
glass and cold walls, glimmer
of something larger. But that's too easy
a figure of order and power. A city
is many bodies, moving, touching,
talking, gathered together, a place
where differences matter and meet,
a song written to the beat of many feet.

~

In the neighborhood assessment, the teacher
asks us to think about how bodies
move, how and where they go.

How many banks or payday lenders
within a mile of your house, she says,
how many grocery stores, libraries, schools?
These are moral questions. How far
is health care from where you are,
if you had no car? Are there
sidewalks where you live? She turns
her hands up as she asks—as if
they could be filled. What can people do?
What do they have access to?

~

Sometimes, the prophet says, your body
is your only weapon, he says,
you put your body in the street
to say what needs be said. Sometimes,
he says, you tuck your body in
so the wheels don't turn. You hold
your hand up, empty. You lift
your hand above your eyes, as if
to shade the sun, as if you're looking
into the distance, when you're just
looking to the future, for what's
not yet here. Hold your hand out
to someone—we do it all the time—
consider how we greet each other
in handshake or bro hug, fist bump
or bussed cheek, what we do
when we meet, the grammar of hands
and bodies, of who we are and what
we think of one another. A mass
of bodies is saying something—
whether it's a market shutting
down Main, a dinner on a bridge,
a great crowd of witnesses watching
a flag come down, or maybe a room
of people sitting together, listening
to a man who asks them to imagine

themselves part of one body,
one city, one place,
sharing each other's fate.

~

Our city lifts its hand to shade its eyes.
Our city wants to see into the distance.
Our city does not turn its back.
Our city does not hog the table.
Our city knows everyone is disabled in some way.
Our city offers a hand, opens a door.
Our city likes to talk.
Our city would rather build a bridge than build a wall.
Our city wants to hear your story.
Our city leans to listen.
Our city knows its soul is filled by art.
Our city sets a light out when it's dark.
Our city is not a clenched fist.
Our city does not turn its back.
Our city never says I alone can fix it.
Our city knows we only get there together.
Our city wipes its brow, gets to work.

Crossing

Written for the 2017 Gervais Street Bridge Dinner, October 22, 2017.

Back then, crossing over was an event—
the bridge told you so, its arches and fancy
lanterns—time moved on below you. Crossing

over meant becoming someone, a different
being headed to a different place. Of course
Sherman had burned an earlier one. Back then,

you could get off the trolley at the Richland end
of the Gervais Street bridge, walk up the canal
to Irwin Park on Laurel, with its tiny zoo

and its view of the state penitentiary, a park
blacks could use only on Tuesdays and Thursdays—
so many ways to lock things up, block things

off, like dropping rocks on the toxic sludge
of coal tar that leaked back then and now lines
the river bottom from here down to Blossom.

Turn the tap and take a glass of water.
Imagine it, the whole watershed distilled
into eight clear ounces in your hand,

filtered first by the mussels before it ever
reaches a treatment plant, the slabshells
and heelsplitters, the pink rayed fatmucket.

Upstream, rivers of traffic now converge
on the I-26 bridge, slow down to sluggish
in the daily rush, and we're lucky if we even turn

soon enough to see the great blue heron
like an origami trick, a cantankerous kite,
unfolding itself into flight against the sky.

Postcard: Columbia Canal

At the top of the canal the lock
is a clogged mat of debris—three
mylar balloons floating with the flood
flotsam, the plastic bottles. The river
curls over the low dam, froths on
the rocks below. The canal is still
as a slough, a mirror, desilvering.

survivor

March for Science, South Carolina State House, April 22, 2017

suburban deer pause in the empty lot next
door ears up bodies rigid in the light someone
leaves corn out for them they follow
the scent the creek to the river clatter
across asphalt streets at night eat the day-
lilies the kale the limelight hydrangeas one
day we find a fawn curled in the long grass
leaning not yet a lien the county will levy
against an absentee owner somewhere
glaciers calving caving carving themselves
off Antarctica *where have you been where
would you go* the calves drifting north a fawn
loping down Elm Abode's not yet busy daylit

streets we will not know it will not notice
will not know that it is not the catastrophe we
expected though no less catastrophic hardly
hardy orchids budded at winter's end not
ended white blooms the cold browns we
discover an armadillo burrowed beneath
the roses my mom says she's never seen
them this far north before the gold spiders
gilding the air between the oaks mosquitoes
not killed not cold enough the cherry weeping

too early somewhere it's *Survivor* another
season another immunity challenge somewhere
steam rising off pools of pale blue water
laced with boron and spent fuel rods resting
at the bottom a great desert ditch bristles
with warning cobalt blue yuccas modified
to blue like test tubes of blue blood bled
from horseshoe crabs *Limulus polyphemus* or
the one-eyed monster that sees the world

askew collected and bled for medicine and
released back to the sea most survive only
a third die the yuccas are modified to mark
the ridge the ditch the hot spot for millennia
to come

Semi

March 23, 2018

On toy assault rifles
you can buy for kids
there is a fake safety

switch to teach kids
how to toggle between
safe, semi, and fully

automatic. The safety
switch is integrated
into the mode switch,

safety being not a
condition or lock, just
another mode of use.

Each gun has a red tip
so that any cop
seeing the gun raised—

even, presumably, from
a great distance—will know
that it's a fake. On toy

assault rifles the safety
switch is molded on
the gun rather than being

an operative switch, a lever
that is forever on *semi*,
stuck between *auto* and *safe*,

a preset permanent mode
of being semi-safe.

Prayer

at the emergency room

for the lights, the charts
for hands and hearts

for those who heal
for those who are healed

for the time it takes

for those who listen
and those who watch

for those who care
for those we care for

for all those here

On considering the bronze bust of J. Marion Sims at the northwest corner of the South Carolina State House grounds

Written for MEND, a poetry marathon to advance the removal of the J. Marion Sims Monument at the South Carolina State House, September 7, 2017.

after Bettina Judd and Kwoya Fagin Maples

"That a historical figure existed at a different time, with different norms, is not irrelevant. But it is only one consideration in the fraught and important question, as to who should loom over us on pedestals, enshrined in metal or stone."
    Ross Andersen on responses to statues of Sims, The Atlantic, *6 Sept 2017*

"The first surgeon of the ages in ministry to women, treating alike empress and slave."
    from the left panel of the Sims monument, SC Statehouse grounds

Because he was not, in fact, physician to empress and slave alike; because he used the bodies of black women and poor women to launch what would become a lucrative practice among wealthy women; because he would not have been physician to an empress in a mansion if he had not first experimented on enslaved women in a shed behind his house;

Because Anarcha and Lucy and Betsy are named as enslaved women in his autobiography but are never given voice;

Because he says of Betsy that "she willingly consented";

Because he invented 71 instruments to aid in childbirth, yes, but because he started with a pewter spoon and a cobbler's awl; because an awl is a long spike used for piercing leather; because this monument remembers the Sims position and the Sims speculum, but it does not remember the shoemaker's tool that he used to pry the bones of a newborn African infants' skulls into proper alignment; because the fatality rate for those operations was 100 percent;

Because he did not use anesthesia on black women; because he was sure they could endure the pain; because they thought blacks had a higher tolerance for pain; because the pain was so great, he asked other men to hold them down;

Because he whitewashed his woodcuts of black women's bodies when he moved to New York, so his patrons and students there would not know that he experimented on the bodies of enslaved women;

Because this monument was erected in May 1929 by the Women's Auxiliary of the South Carolina Medical Association; because the most popular radio show in American in 1929 was *Amos 'n' Andy*; because Martin Luther King Jr. was born four months before in Georgia;

Because the elegant cement curve of the steps of the Sims monument, and the wall broken by the bust of J. Marion Sims so ironically echo the elegant curve of the African American History Monument across the South Carolina Statehouse grounds, a wall of images broken by the historical fissure of the Emancipation Proclamation;

Because the bronze bust of J. Marion Sims, his disembodied head and chest, suggests that this is a monument to reason and affection and not to the bodies of the enslaved women on whom he established his reputation—disappeared, disavowed, but not disowned;

Because he stopped at a store and bought a spoon and then he stopped at his office and called out to his students, "Come, boys, go to the hospital with me"; because a jaunty "Come, boys, go with me" is the story of the invention of the speculum;

Because he performed clitoridectomies on women, because hysteria and improper sexual behavior were pathologized as gynecological illnesses;

Because he says Betsy "willingly consented";

Because consent no longer means the consent of your owner;

Because consent no longer means the consent of your husband;

Because when you stand in front of the bust of J. Marion Sims, he looks down on you, on us, looks down on this mixed crowd; because when you stand in front of the bust of J. Marion Sims, he can't quite look you in the eye;

Because the elliptical arch around this disembodied head suggests a cartouche, suggests the hieroglyphic oval enclosing a royal name, suggests the halo arching over an image of a saint;

Because even though some say the history of J. Marion Sims may be nuanced and complex, this monument is not;

Because getting rid of a monument is not the same thing as erasing history; because the installation of a monument is not an accurate representation of history but an elevation of a particular representation, a particular representative, a particular reduction of history;

Because we should continue to teach the history of J. Marion Sims, his 71 instruments, his bent spoon, his shoemaker's awl; because we should teach the names of Betsy, and Lucy, and Anarcha; because we should say the names;

Window and wall, on Blue Sky's *Tunnelvision* (1975)

Written for the January 30, 2018 State of the City address by Mayor Stephen K. Benjamin.

> "Cities have awakened to the urgent need of a systematic plan for [the] future."
> Harlan Kelsey & Irvin Guild, *The Improvement of Columbia, South Carolina* (1905)

It took nine months of work.

Painting the wall, he carved out a tunnel, hung the sun in front of us.

Nine white overhead lights lead us through the tunnel to the other side.

The details of the mural trick the eye, the real stone merging with the fake, the real metal barriers beside the painted traffic signs.

> *We did not deem it desirable, at this time,* said Kelsey & Guild in 1905, *to place too much emphasis upon detail, because, in doing so, the main objects sought might easily be lost sight of.*

The things that seem to block the way are the things that make you see.

The real windows on the wall look fake, become part of the painting: the vision of what's beyond is the point.

In 1976, *People* magazine called the image "a brilliant orange sunset." *The State* newspaper later called it "a descending sun."

It is not clear, really, if the sun is rising or setting.

> *It is quite possible,* Kelsey & Guild admitted, *that this report will be more useful in its suggestions than in the plan outlined.*

Two white arrows show both lanes going forward, no one is headed back.

My first few weeks in Columbia, a friend drove me over to see it, early evening, the moment the tunnel seems most real, as if you could drive into it.

The sun is the same size as a yellow traffic sign that warns of a right turn ahead, the road curving away and out of sight.

Forty years ago, he warned us of a hard swerve to the right, something we couldn't yet see.

> *The South Carolina Encyclopedia* reminds us that Kelsey and Guild's proposals were too ambitious to receive serious consideration, but they set a precedent for comprehensive planning.

Blue Sky told *People* magazine, *I wanted to reach through that wall, touch something larger than life.*

Rumor is a kid once drove right into the mural.

The things that block the way must be the things that help you see.

The wall was a way out. The windows are dark.

There is a hard swerve to the right, we can't see what's there.

The sun is shining in front of us.

Better angels

Written for the January 29, 2019 State of the City address by Mayor Stephen K. Benjamin.

Hanging on my sister-in-law's wall
is a print we've all seen: an angel
hovering over two kids walking across
a rickety bridge, kids sure to fall

if she weren't there—there's a board
missing at their feet, the rail gone
on one side. The poor kids are barefoot,
the girl's got a basket, she's got her arm

round the boy's shoulder. Neither sees
the angel, who floats above the bridge, lightning
in the distance. The angel reaches out
as if she's blocking trouble on either side,

as if she wants to gather them up in her arms
and wrap them in her robes. She hovers over,
unable to do either. In 1861,
Lincoln asked his secretary of state

for help with his first inaugural address.
South Carolina had already done its part
to start butchering up the map of who we
were, and it was about to get worse.

What could he say, given the state of the union?
Sewell was glad to help, gave the president
seven pages of suggestions and wrote up
something pretty for the end, calling on

the guardian angel of the nation.

~

Lincoln didn't use that phrase.
Instead, he said, *mystic chords*

of memory would swell a chorus of unity,
of union once again, if touched, he said,

as surely they will be, by
the better angels of our nature.

No, for Lincoln, the answer wasn't
some agent, some angel outside us

or beyond, but here, among us, within us.
He wasn't thinking about angels

and demons sitting on our shoulders.
He was thinking about a message,

something we can almost hear
now, a century and a half later.

~

In the empty lot next door, daffodils
are coming up—a message from the past,
drawing the lines of a house no longer there.

That image of the guardian angel was first
a German postcard. The print in my in-law's home
hangs in homage to a Mississippi grandma,

who'd hung it with a light shining on it.
In ancient scripture, an angel was just a messenger—
sometimes divine, sometimes human—the same

word, *mal'ākh*, same task. Scripture tells us
when we feed the hungry, welcome the stranger,
whatever we do to the poorest among us, we do

to the divine in all of us. Is that her brother?
Is that his sister? Am I my brother's keeper?
What's in her basket? Loaves and fishes?

What if the boy wore a hoodie and carried
a bag of Skittles? What if they were tired
and tongue-tied kids wrapped in silver

blankets? What if she were wearing a hijab?
What if he were wearing a prayer cap?
Or what if he already knows his difference, hers,

and they will come back to that bridge
years later to look down into the dark?
The angel hovering over is not the angel

of history, winds of catastrophe caught in her wings,
blowing her back. No, she's looking at what's
in front, not what's behind them. The angel wants

to fix the bridge, the missing step, the broken
rail, but she knows she can't. To do that
takes something better. It takes human hands.

Song

A bike goes by. Someone sings
with earbuds in, a song we know.
Listen: the sound of water and wind
and faint, below all birdsong and gurgle,
the insistent thrum of time. Trees
scatter leaves at mudside, on wave.
You throw a stone. It skips and sinks,
the way the river takes us all.

Not just a collar

Written for the memorial for Supreme Court Justice Ruth Bader Ginsburg on the steps of the SC State Supreme Court, September 24, 2020.

A collar is not just a collar—one thing
they taught us, Ginsburg and O'Connor in jabots
of lace, staking a place among the men
all in collar and tie. Ginsberg saw
the Constitution as a document of promise,
not privilege. She said that even when
you change the players, separate but equal is still
not equal, the field's not level, and as long
as laws rely on unproven assumptions
about the way women are, those laws
keep women in their place, not
on a pedestal but in a cage. And whether
or not a surviving parent is mom or dad,
the child is still a child and it should be
apparent that a parent is still a parent.
And whether or not that Arizona girl
had a pill in her pocket at school, the men
in the room need to consider how it would feel
to be strip-searched for Ibuprophen
as a 13-year-old girl. She won that one
but sometimes it's not about winning here
and now, but in a distant there and then
when women have the same opportunities
as men.

    If a collar is not just a collar,
a jabot may be both job and jab,
the lace meticulous, precise, knots
and links like the inky lace of letters
on a page. She says her college lit professor
taught her that the right words in the right
order matter, that words can paint a picture.

If a South Carolina law had caused the court
to say a blight of racism infects the body
politic, she said it had become more
like the Hydra, the monster snake Hercules
fought that grew new heads every time
he cut one off. Every time a racist
election law was identified and stopped,
she said, "others sprang up in its place,"
like Texas trying to disenfranchise Blacks
by passing the same law over and over
again. The other judges pretended that,
as Roberts said, "things have changed dramatically."
She said, instead, that throwing out something
when it has worked and is continuing to work
to stop discrimination "is like throwing
away your umbrella in a rainstorm because
you are not getting wet." The right
words in the right order. When rioters
were banging on the glass doors of a Florida
election office with clipboards and fists in order
to shut down the recount in *Bush v. Gore*,
she was a dogged defender of proper procedure,
even if it meant delay in naming a president.
It was then she dropped "respectfully" from
the usual close, writing instead, *I dissent*.

The court, she said, does not write on a clean
slate. Things accumulate, persist, like mercury
in a river in Rocbuck, South Carolina,
even after the company changed their name
to Safety-Kleen, then finally closed the plant.
It's all moot, they said, since they had
cleaned up their act, though it wasn't clear
they wouldn't do it again. Or like the pay
raises Lilly Ledbetter received, small
increments that deceived her for years. Other
judges pretended that "each and every pay
decision she did not immediately challenge

wiped the slate clean." Yet those decisions,
together, set and kept her pay well below
every other manager.

      There is no
clean slate. There's only history, precedent,
the blurred and half-erased words we write
over. In '73 Ginsburg urged the Court
to recognize that it writes not only for
"this case and this day alone" but other
cases like it, and others to come, asking—
whether a state cherishes its daughters as much
as its sons, whether a schoolgirl has got
a pill in her pocket or not, whether a raise
is really a raise when it's all added up.

A few years ago the justice wrote, "Dissents
speak to a future age. . . . That's the dissenter's
hope: that they are writing not for today,
but for tomorrow." A collar is not just
a collar. When Ginsburg opened her office closet
for Katie Couric, it was a glossary, a semiotics
of gift, event, decision. And when she wore
that spiky rhinestone-studded number she got
from *Glamour*, we knew it meant: *I dissent*.

No, not spikes but 20-something dark
and dazzling tongues, ruthless, speaking not
quite as one but pointed, speaking up
and speaking out, speaking against, against,
dissenting, not for today, but for tomorrow.

Fireflies, Congaree National Park

on photo postcards by Sean Rayford, Soda Citizen Post Card Club

1.

The night vibrates
with so many songs.

Almost the Fourth
and the fireflies tonight

are fireworks enough.

2.

Fireflies are
       sparks
                drifting from

                                     a cold fire,

the dust
       of exploded
                                     stars,

small words written on the dark.

A table big enough

a poem to welcome a delegation from Nigeria to Columbia, August 2, 2021

A few years ago, a friend came
from overseas. He was disappointed,
he said, that my porch was so small,
room for just one chair to watch
the road, only a small table for
a book, a glass. He wanted there to be
a big porch like the ones he'd seen
on tv, that version of who we were,
who he thought we might still be.

I remember once, in Brazil, a drive
through the dark, a hospital briefly flashed
up and then only more darkness.
The van was hot, the stars were hid.
The roads got smaller, rougher, the van
slowed, stopped beside a wall. Someone
rung a bell, a gate swung open. We were
exhausted. I don't know what we expected.
Someone walked us across the courtyard.
We could hear people talking, a language
we barely understood, if at all.
We went in, a bright room.

I said to my disappointed friend,
there is a fountain at the door, and every
morning the small birds visit. At night,
feral cats, sometimes deer. And here,
I said, the big trees spread shade
like a carpet. Once a car pulled up
beside the big magnolia at the corner.
A woman stepped out. She didn't see me.
She stood there, smelling the flowers, then
broke one off, got back in her car and drove

away. I would've given it to her
if she had asked, I said, there were still
so many blooms. I took my friend round back,
where there were two chairs, a table
big enough for us, two glasses, a shared
plate, and near enough the door to fetch
anything we needed. We sat and talked.
He said, the world is bigger than we thought.
I said, it's smaller than we know.

That night in Brazil, a late dinner
had been left out for us, pitchers of water,
and better, coconuts tonsured like monks
and wearing straws. We sat, talking, around
a large table—room enough for all of us.
Someone translated, we said what we could,
we listened. We moved to the long porch
for the breeze, walked out into the dark
to see the stars, each of us adjusting
our inner clocks—the times of where we
had been—all of us now standing under
the same stars, the world being smaller
than we thought, bigger than we know.

~

Let the trees spread their shade for you.
Let the table be big enough for all.
Let us say what we can to one another.
Let us listen.

Let there be plates that we can share.
Let there be pitchers of cold water.
Let the stars teach us how small we are.
Let us learn.

Help us to learn the words of welcome—
the *how you dey*, the *e ku abo*,
the *sannu*, the *nnọọ*.

The world is bigger than we thought.
The world is smaller than we thought.
Let our hearts be bigger than we know.

V

When you look back, what do you see?

> *"The future is never set in stone. Remember that."*
> *Isobel in* The Night Circus

Lot's wife looked back, she turned to salt.
Some say it was because she asked

her neighbors for salt, so they knew she was
hosting strangers. Some say the loss

of what she left behind seized her, some
that she was just making sure her daughters

were following. Some say she looked back
and was stunned by what she saw—fire,

light, the way that we are tossed and mauled
by forces larger than us, the great churning

sea in which our lives are small, sweet
accidents, like the bright yellow tomatoes

that reseeded and returned a second summer,
or the blue mist flower that never

announces its flowering—you walk out one
morning and see its small pale constellations.

Two clocks on the same street

Written for the January 29, 2020 State of the City address by Mayor Stephen K. Benjamin.

There is never only one clock.
Even here, there are two, and both
must be wound by hand since time isn't
just the turn of sun or season or
the binary beat of your watch but
someone's hand long ago turning
a key, a crank, so that everybody got
to work and trains mostly ran on time.

There is never only one clock.
Even here, there are two, and both
have four faces, as if the tempo of Main
Street changes from one block to another,
as if those going north toward city hall
see time differently from those headed
south to the statehouse, where stories
congeal into marble, even when
they're not quite true. It depends
on where you stand. Whether you are
in front of the jewelry store or
the bank, the art museum or the coffee
shop, the hotel or the dorm, the Brazilian
steakhouse where the attendant is parking
your car, or the water department, where
you're standing in line to pay your bill.
The clock of someone waiting at a bus
stop is different from the clock of a man
driving a car, which is different from
the clock running out at the end
of a game. The coffee shop is in one
time zone, the hospital another, and they
are only blocks from each other.

There is never only one clock.
There is the clock on the wall, the clock
on your wrist, and all the clocks embedded
in our flesh. There is the clock of the river,
which measures its banks, and the clock
of pollen, which slows us all down
until the rains wash the air. There is
the clock of stoplights, the clock of school
buses. There is the sun clock and the moon
clock, the circulations of feral cats,
the visitations of migrating birds, the orb
spiders hanging shimmering clocks in autumn
air, and the strange and beautiful clock
of fireflies synchronizing themselves with one
another. And it is not always clear
how these synch with the clock of council
meetings or the replacement of street lights
or parking meters or artwork at the airport.

There are two clocks on the same street.
Time is the circle of the sun over
the river, seeing the same things again
but in a slightly different light, and time
is also the wavy line of the river
beneath the sun, always moving on.

January is a clock with two faces
facing opposite ways. One hand
waves a flag of corn and cotton, as if
here we think we're still there, in a past
that was small and unfair, where justice
might have been the queen of virtues, but
someone kept her blindfolded. The other
hand unfurls something like a wing,
a wave, a page about to be turned
at last. And a decade is just another
way to say the train depot is not
a depot, the post office is no longer

a post office, the park was something else,
and a bank has slapped its logo over
the shoulder of the statehouse. A decade is
a way to draw a dark line through all
the little changes, not a clock but
the shadow of a bridge over the ripples
of the river, to say look at what all
has happened between there and here.

Then: pandemic postcards

1. Shutdown

The peach tree, tall as me, is blooming.
So is the quince, so are the tulips,

and there's a dust of pollen sifted
across it all. In a month it will be

Easter, but for now spring break
had been extended an extra week

because of the virus. I wave
at a family walking by together, a safe

distance away. We'll call our neighbor
later, make sure she's okay. A friend

says his Christmas cactus is confused,
posts a photo of a pot of red blooms,

then adds, *but aren't we all these days.*

2. Resilient, after *Man Lying with Branch* **by Anselm Kiefer**

He lay down in the cold.
He was tired of that word—
resilient. He wasn't. He felt
a sorrow growing from
his chest, the limbs of it
shaking in the cold wind,
and, yes, the thorns.

3. Coffee with a friend

We bump elbows, unsure,
assure each other we're
after vaccination and before

we know it, we've slipped off
the spacesuits we've worn
for months, fear-equipped,

and fall back into old orbits,
habits, laughter, touching
the same little jug of milk.

At the Most Worshipful Prince Hall Grand Lodge

early voting, Columbia, SC, October 31, 2020

Across the parking lot, a man with a mic
is calling out *drop, pop, and roll,* and two
women just in front of us in line dance
along. It's getting a little festive, a little
restless as we get closer to the door,
where they let in six or seven at a time.
One woman shuffles the heel-toe in fluffy
pink house shoes. They name the moves,
call out a few they don't think quite right.

A golfcart bumps by with boxes of popcorn.
A church offers bottled waters at a table
where the line curls along the back fence.
It's been a two-hour wait. We got here early
enough, but the line was already around
the building. Everyone is wearing masks except
a middle-aged white couple in black and
sunglasses, taking occasional deep pulls
on their electric cigarettes. Most of us look

at our cellphones as we wait, another
kind of social distance. The line wraps
around the building then coils around
an adjacent parking lot. An old woman
leaves crying because the county isn't
providing provisional ballots for early voting
sites. I don't know why. Once inside
we line up on the thick strips of gray
tape that mark off the floor. A poll worker

behind a plastic shield stares at my license
a bit—I can't tell if she's comparing
signatures or if it's just the COVID hair. Finally,

she hands me a slip of paper, a cotton swab,
points me toward the wall of voting machines.
I use the cotton swab to touch the screen.
I get an "I Voted" sticker when I leave.

Crossing the borders

a poem of welcome, May 2022

It is hard to know what we don't know.
We know so little about one another.

I tell my mother a story. She listens at first. It is
a version of what's going on in the world.

But then she sees the journal on the table, or I
mention the channel the story was on, and she is then

suspicious of the story I tell. My grandmother says
she can't talk about politics with her friends

because they all assume that she believes what
they believe, assume she listens to the same

news, but she doesn't. We read what we can.
All the new stories seem to confirm the old

ways of thinking. How do we cross the border of one
story and enter another? How do I weigh one story

against another, which may be similar, may not, but is
still someone's way of seeing the world? Imagine

we are in the airport, maybe checking in
with the baggage we carry as we move from one

place to another, or sitting at the gates,
ready to go, or maybe having coffee, listening

for a voice we understand. It is crowded.
Someone sits at our table. *Where are you going,*

we ask, or *where have you been?* Each question invites
a story. On the screens above us, the pundits

are testing out accounts that can harden hearts,
stories more or less true. If we are wearing masks,

we can take them off here. Let's stay here
a while, tell each other what we know, maybe

learn a little about what we don't. So many
arrivals, so many departures, so many stories,

some condensed, abridged, interpreted, more
or less true, versions stamped and approved

by the gatekeepers, everyone carrying what
they need to make sense of the world. Tell me

what you carry, I will tell you what I carry.
Maybe, together, we can work out what is true.

Aboard

I marched the animals in, tumbled
in a jumble of limbs, tossed on the waves.

I marched the animals out: a parade.
It was my favorite toy as a child,

a barn that was a boat, a door
to open when the flood receded.

A crow flew over: my hand the crow.
A dove flew over: my hand the dove.

I spread them out across the floor,
my room the world saved again.

~

The sky is filled with crows.
The sea is filled with teeth.

~

What is the world but an ark—

not a bank not a mall not a mine (and not mine, or yours)
not a garden not a market not an all-you-can-eat buffet

but an ark floating in a cold dark sea.
No, on seas warming inexorably.

~

Someone looks behind   counting.
Someone looks ahead   longing.

Someone watches for the signs—
the crow, the dove with a new leaf in its beak.

Our hands: the crows.
Our hands: the doves.

Postcard: Boyd Greenhouse

Hampton-Preston Mansion, 2022

The glass house is a sketch of line
and light across the back lawn,
blue in the day's glare, at night
like a lit vitrine of another time—
what grew here, what could grow,
a crate of air and expectation.

Flag

a poem for the adoption of the new City of Columbia flag, March 10, 2020

A leaf, a wing, a sail,
something lifted, lifting,
something new. What

does it mean, he asks.
By which she means, *what
do you see?* Three

rivers come together.
A road stretches toward
horizon—a lane of light,

of white, into the distance,
which is the future, a lane
of blue to remind you of sky

and water, and who we were.
The shadow of hills flares
against the sky, or forests,

another blue beyond us,
and beyond that a light
in a dark sky, a guide,

talisman, beacon, star.
The horizon is who we are.

Postcard: jimson weed

We stuck a few unopened blooms
of jimson in the bouquet we gave
the host. During dinner they
unfurled—the perfume filled the room.
Cut off from where we grew,
sometimes, still, we open.

Notes

The poems are arranged roughly but not consistently in chronological order. Most of the official occasions for which the poems were written are noted in the text, but some additional contexts are provided below.

"On a tour of the state house grounds": After the death of SC Senator Strom Thurmond in 2003, Essie Mae Washington-Williams revealed that Thurmond was her biological father, making public the long-rumored secret that the segregationist politician was the father of a biracial daughter. Her mother was Carrie Butler—at the time of her birth, a 16-year-old African American girl working as a domestic servant in the home of Thurmond's parents. Thurmond was 22 and unmarried. In 2004, the South Carolina legislature approved the addition of Washington's name to the list of children on the statue of Thurmond on the State House grounds and "father of four children" was changed to "five."

"Stars": The epigraph is taken from William Faulkner's *Absalom, Absalom!*: "We don't live among defeated grandfathers and freed slaves [. . .] and bullets in the dining room table and such, to be always reminding us to never forget." The six bronze stars affixed to the west and southwest walls of the State House mark where the building was hit by Union artillery fired from across the Congaree River on February 19, 1865.

"From the ashes": The lines in italics are taken from *Sherman and the Burning of Columbia* by historian Marion Brunson Lucas (1976).

"Walk back through the ashes": Written during the week of programming for the Burning of Columbia in February 2015, this poem draws imagery from dance and other public performances during the commemoration.

"Hercules and the wagoner": The oldest independent African Methodist Episcopal (AME) church in the American South, Mother Emanuel AME in Charleston, SC, was the site of a horrific shooting on June 17, 2015, when a young white man murdered nine people attending Bible study. In 1822, white Charlestonians burned the original church to the ground after one of the church's founders, Denmark Vesey, was accused and convicted of organizing a revolt of enslaved people. It was rebuilt after the Civil War. The 2015 murder marked a turning point in public and political opinion about the flying of the Confederate battle flag over the state capitol.

"Postcard: First Baptist Church, Columbia, S.C.": As a daily creative practice and a public arts project in 2022, I wrote a draft of a poem every day on a postcard, which was posted to social media and mailed. Some of the postcards, such as this one, were of historic scenes in Columbia and South Carolina.

"When we're told we'll never understand": Many lines in this poem are taken from news reports and social media in the days following the shooting. The title comes from a statement by then SC Governor Nikki Haley, who said, "We do know that we'll never understand what motivates anyone to enter one of our places of worship and take the life of another," a comment seen by many as a refusal to acknowledge the racism of the act and the culture that enabled it. I am grateful to then Columbia City Councilman Moe Baddourah, who said to me after the shooting, "You're the city laureate. You should say something." In my first year as the city's laureate, this was a charge to think beyond ceremonial poems and to say something with a public voice, to take advantage of the voice and the post I had been given. I am also grateful to local poet Al Black, who read the poem at the Take It Down rally (urging the removal of the Confederate battle flag from the state house) on June 20, 2015.

"Remember" was written for the 2015 Poems on the Comet project, the first of six installations of poems by local poets on the Midlands area transit buses.

"Sweep" was written for the interdisciplinary and inter-arts project Marked by the Water, a response to the historic floods organized by *Jasper* editor Cindi Boiter. The poem was later incorporated into a dance performance by The Power Company, directed by Martha Brim.

"The lesson that night" was written in response to an invitation from *The State* newspaper to write a poem one year after the Charleston shooting. The poem was published on the front page of the paper, superimposed over a photograph of the Mother Emanuel church steeple. The poem was also read at the gallery opening for The Holy City: Art of Love, Unity, & Resurrection, Charleston, May 29, 2017. In addition to the Charleston shooting, the poem refers to a 2016 incident in which a young African American female student was thrown from her desk and dragged by a resource officer at Spring Valley High School in Columbia and to the 2015 murder of Walter Scott in Charleston, a Black man shot in the back by a police officer.

"Postcard: Lincoln Street Tunnel," originally titled "Cave," was written for the annual chalk art festival, ArtLinc, October 26, 2019, where it was combined with chalk illustration by Bert Easter.

"On a photograph of student protestors" was written in response to a photograph that is part of the Columbia63 project (http://www.columbiasc63.com/timeline/student-activism/). An earlier version of this poem was written to celebrate Black History Month and college leadership and read at the Benedict College President's Dinner, February 10, 2015.

"The sound of a needle on vinyl" was also read for the launch of Stormwater Studios during the Artista Vista festival, April 19, 2018.

"Pollen": The poem was part of a collaboration with writer Alexis Stratton for Identity, a Columbia Museum of Art Community Gallery Exhibition organized by Leslie Pierce, in conjunction with the 2015 Andy Warhol exhibit, *From Marilyn to Mao: Andy Warhol's Famous Faces*.

"Postcard: Main Street," originally titled "Perspective," was included in the 2018 Poems on the Comet project focused on the theme "Two Cities," poems on things that divide us, things that unite us.

"Translations": In 2021, official Irish dictionaries were changed to recognize the use of *duine de dhath*, or person of color. The language in italics is taken from "Lotus: Showing the Way to Enlightenment," by Amy Chavez. I am grateful to my former students Caleb Coker and Devon Sherrell for conversations and emails that enriched this poem and my own understanding.

"Nothing is perfect, everything is beautiful": A visual artist and director of adult programs and partnerships at the Columbia Museum of Art, Leslie Pierce passed away on June 28, 2015. In 2011, she and her friend and collaborator Alejandro Garcia Lémos organized a show centered on the image of Saint Sebastian. The poem was written for and read at her memorial service.

"Something to declare" was written with students at the Tri-District Arts Consortium summer arts camp, after we read William Stafford's poem of the same title.

"Which" was included in the 2020 Poems on the Comet, poems about time, a theme that seemed particularly relevant during the pandemic shutdown.

"Sherman sonata": Phrases in third section are taken from biographies of General W.T. Sherman and accounts of the February 1865 burning of Columbia, SC—Marion Brunson Lucas's *Sherman and the Burning of Columbia* (1976); Miram Freeman Rawl's *From the Ashes of Ruin* (1999), Anne Sarah Rubin's *Through the Heart of Dixie: Sherman's March and American Memory* (2014), Richard Wheeler's *Sherman's March* (1978), and especially Lee Kennett's *Sherman: A Soldier's Life* (2001).

"A new year" is for Coralee Harris (1954-2017).

"Body politic" was also read at the 2017 City of Columbia's Mayor's Bike and Walk Summit: Planning for a More Accessible City at It-ology, May 4, 2017.

"Crossing" is for poet John Lane, who writes about our rivers, and for Congaree Riverkeeper Bill Stangler, who protects them. "Postcard: Columbia Canal" is also for Stangler.

"survivor" was written for and read at the March for Science at the State House, April 22, 2017.

"Semi" is taken from a longer text, part of an installation titled In Guns We Trust that was mounted in the front window of Tapp's Art Center, March 18, 2018, in advance of the March for Our Lives Rally, March 23, 2018, organized to protest gun violence. Like many simultaneous marches nationwide, the protest was organized in response to the shooting at Stoneman Douglas High School in Parkland, Florida, February 14, 2018. The installation was later included in A Dialogue of Black and White, a collection of protest and political art exhibited at City Gallery in Charleston.

"Prayer": This poem was published untitled on the Emergency Care Guides in the Prisma Health System in the

Midlands (Columbia and Sumter), at the invitation of an arts and poetry committee organized by Dawn Hill at Prisma Health and my former student, Alexandra Toney. A short video account of the project can be found at For All Those Here: Poetry in Unexpected Places at Prisma Health (https://www.youtube.com/watch?v=MH_IctUc_pY). The project was launched on July 17, 2019.

"On considering the bronze bust of J. Marion Sims at the northwest corner of the South Carolina State House" was written for Mend, a marathon six-hour reading calling for the monument's removal, which took place in front of the monument on September 7, 2017. I am grateful to the organizers, especially Joy Priest and Trez Len, for the invitation to read. I felt both awkward and humbled as the only white reader at an event intended as meditation on black female experience. I am also grateful to poets Bettina Judd, who read at USC in February 2016, and Kwoya Fagin Maples, who organized and anchored this protest reading. Their poetry offers a rich interrogation of this history. A note on the form: I had in mind the series of "because" or "whereas" clauses that often structure a formal resolution. The poem does not end, however, with "be it resolved," since there is no resolution yet to advance the monument's removal or to correct its misleading "historical" account.

"Window and wall, on Blue Sky's *Tunnelvision*": Boston landscape architects Harlan Kelsey and Irvin Guild drew up the 88-page plan, *The Improvement of Columbia, South Carolina* (1905), at the request of the Columbia Civic League. The report emphasized long-term vision—"working on broad lines and with far-seeing eyes." At present Blue Sky's mural has limited public visibility as the wall is less accessible, the parking lot now blocked by the gates and barriers of private parking—an unintended but useful comment on the importance of vision and planning suggested by both his mural and the 1905 study.

"Song" was written for Poems on the Comet 2017, the theme of rivers.

"Not just a collar": The poem refers to a number of cases central to the career of Supreme Court Justice Ruth Bader Ginsburg, including the first case she argued before the Supreme Court, *Frontiero v. Richardson* (1973); also *Weinberger v. Wiesenfeld* (1975); the South Carolina environmental lawsuit *Friends of the Earth, Inc. v. Laidlaw Environmental Services, Inc.* (2000); *Ledbetter v. Goodyear Tire and Rubber Company* (2007); *Safford Unified School District v. Redding* (2009); the voter suppression case *Shelby County v. Holder* (2013); and, of course, *Bush v. Gore* (2000), the case in which she removed the decorous "respectfully" from "I dissent."

"A table big enough" was written to welcome a delegation of social activists from Nigeria to the South Carolina State House on August 2, 2021. This was the first of a series of poems written at the invitation of the Columbia Council for Internationals to welcome international visitors in the city for State Department sponsored forums. In the summer of 2022, I also wrote "Crossing the borders," a welcome poem for a delegation from Eastern Europe focusing on countering disinformation in older adults, and "Aboard," a poem that was translated into Spanish for delegates from South American discussing environmental resilience and climate change. I am grateful to Sewell Gelberd for these invitations. Columbia was the only city out of 84 in the nation to greet delegates with a poem by the city laureate.

"When you look back, what do you see?" is for Cindi Boiter. A longer version was written for the occasion of her birthday.

"Two clocks on the same street": There are two street clocks on Columbia's Main Street. At the corner of Main and Hampton stands the Sylvan Brothers jewelry store clock, installed in 1906. An almost identical clock was installed later a block away and across the street at the corner of Main and Washington.

"Then": Part 1 was read as "Spring break 2020" for the Richland Library On the Road: Poetry Fix Edition online video, April 16, 2020. Part 2, "Resilient," was posted as part of the 2022 postcard project. Part 3, "Coffee with a friend," was included in Poems on the Comet 2021, on the theme of "When It's Over." It is for Lee Snelgrove.

"Postcard: Boyd Greenhouse" is for Robin Waites and Historic Columbia. The new glass greenhouse, funded by the Darnall W. and Susan F. Boyd Foundation, opened in 2022.

"Postcard: jimson weed" was written for the 2022 Poems on the Comet project, the last of six installations of poems by local poets on the Midlands area transit buses. The theme, "Openings," acknowledged newly elected Mayor Daniel Rickenmann's first public events, where he said that Columbia is a city with open arms for all.

Thanks & Acknowledgments

Grateful acknowledgment is made to the editors of the following publications in which earlier versions of these poems first appeared. Many of these poems also appeared on the poet laureate website, columbiapoet.org, maintained by One Columbia.

Art from the Ashes: Columbia Artists Respond to the Sesquicentennial of the Burning of Their City (Muddy Ford Press, 2015): "Stars"

Cold Mountain Review: "From the ashes" and "Sherman sonata"

Free Times: "When we're told we'll never understand"

The Good Men Project (online): "Red, white, black, or before the eclipse" and "Translations." "Red, white, black or before the eclipse" was selected by the editors as one of the best poems published by GMP in 2017.

Jasper: "At the Gervais Street Bridge Dinner" and "Nothing is perfect, everything is beautiful"

Marked by the Water: Artists Respond to a Thousand Year Flood (Muddy Ford Press, 2016): "Sweep" and "At the Gervais Street Bridge Dinner"

Poems in the Aftermath: An Anthology from the 2016 Presidential Transition Period (Indolent Books, 2017): "The Gates" (as "9th November 2016, The Gates")

The State (Columbia SC): "Better angels," "Body politic," "The lesson that night," and "When we're told we'll never understand"

Ukweli: Searching for Healing, Truth, South Carolina Writers and Poets Explore American Racism (Charleston SC: Evening Post Books, 2022): "The curse"

What Rough Beast (online series, Indolent Books): "A new year," "At the Most Worshipful Prince Hall Grand Lodge, Columbia SC, October 31, 2020," "Semi," and "Something to declare"

"At the Most Worshipful Prince Hall Grand Lodge, Columbia SC, October 31, 2020" was also published as an election day poem on the Jasper Project blog.

~

Eight years as the city's inaugural poet laureate was an extraordinary experience. I am very grateful to One Columbia for Arts & Culture, the original selection committee, and the Columbia City Council, who made this position possible. I am also grateful to former Mayor Steven K. Benjamin, who consistently included me in ceremonial occasions and in the life of the city, and who always let me know something about what he was thinking—a theme, a phrase, a Bible verse—so that my work might somehow echo his presentation. I am also grateful that our city was the first in the state to include the voice of poetry as one of the ways that a city and a community can define and question itself.

For eight amazing years as the city laureate, I am deeply grateful to four people.

I am most grateful to Lee Snelgrove, the director of One Columbia for Arts and Culture, the organization in charge of the poet laureate position. Friend, graphic designer, brainstormer, bartender, he was the best collaborator ever. He knew when to ask permission, and who and how, and also when not to. He created opportunities for me, including me in everything from a dinner under the Elmwood overpass to the burial of a time capsule on North Main to candidates' forums at the Koger Center. He made fake poetry parking tickets that looked like real parking tickets. He introduced me to Carl Wilson's *Let's Talk About Love* (a book that I now regularly teach), and to bluegrass covers on Spotify.

I am also very grateful to my friend Cindi Boiter, *Jasper* magazine and Muddy Ford Press editor, arts organizer, extraordinary hostess, and Jasper Project director. If you are in her circle, all manner of good things flow your way—projects, opportunities, parties—and every event is *an event*. Her work with *Jasper*, which I was excited to be part of, encouraged interdisciplinarity and collaboration and cooperation (and fun), and she has helped to break down disciplinary silos and the town-gown divide that fractured the arts community in this city (though there's always more work to do). She was the engine behind the movement to create the laureate position, and for that and so many other things, I am in her debt.

In my life as a poet, I am also grateful to Ray McManus, my best, most generous and most honest critic. Almost everything I wrote for this position—like almost everything I write—I ran by him. What is better is better because of his suggestions, and what remains pedantic or clunky is mine. He also roped me into multiple young writers' workshops and summer camps.

And always always always, I am grateful to my husband, Bert Easter, who not only supports all that I do, but does what he can to make everything more beautiful. Those metal P-O-E-T-R-Y letters in bright colors on stakes that showed up at one outdoor event after another? Bert. You need tables, tablecloths, bottled water, champagne, someone to set up the chairs or pass out the programs or staff the door or write something fancy in chalk, flowers at the pop-up poetry park? Bert. When we couldn't get a church pew through the door into the Tapp's window for the anti-gun-violence installation, Bert took it apart and put it back together, all hammers and ingenuity and sweat. And love. I could not have done this work without his creativity, his support, and his encouragement.

Indeed, I could not have done this work at all without the support of those four people.

It was also a joy to participate in readings and workshops with the other laureates in the state: Laurel Blossom (Edgefield), Marcus Amaker (Charleston), Jo Angela Edwins (Pee Dee), Angelo Geter (Rock Hill), J. Drew Lanham (Edgefield), and, of course, Marjory Wentworth, the state poet laureate 2003-2020.

I want to express my gratitude to the Academy of American Poets for honoring my public work with one of the inaugural poet laureate fellowships in 2019, especially director Jennifer Benka and programs director Nikay Paredes. It was such a delight to meet other laureates in that cohort of fellows and learn from their work. I am grateful to both the Instituto Sacatar in Itaparica, Brazil, and the Hambidge Center for the Creative Arts in Georgia for residencies where some of these poems were written. I am grateful as well to the College of Arts and Sciences, the Department of English, and the Women's and Gender Studies Program at the University of South Carolina for supporting this work. And to the students in my creative writing and community classes for their own fascinating public poetry projects—especially Lily Heidari, Kwame Kennedy, Susan Swavely, and Alexandra Toney.

I am grateful to Kathryn Kirkpatrick at Appalachian State University and Nathalie Anderson at Swarthmore College for invitations to their campuses that helped me to think more carefully about what it means to have a public voice. Similarly, I am grateful to the opportunity to participate in the Public Affairs Conference at Missouri State University in 2017.

For invitations not already mentioned, I want to thank Benedict College, Martha Brim and the Power Company, Chad Henderson (Vista Queen, Ghostlight), Emile DeFelice (Gervais Street Bridge Dinners, Soda City Market), Tom Hall, Larry Hembree, Jeffrey Makala at Furman University, Jerome Meadows and the Blank Page Poetry project at the 701 Center for Contemporary Art, the Midlands Men's Chorus, Horace Mungin and Herb Frazier, Richland Library (especially Sarah Gough, Phillip Higgins, and Tony Tallent), Tony Snell Rodriguez and SC Pride, Nekki Shutt (Ginsberg memorial), and Cookie Washington in Charleston. Also the Rotary and Kiwanis clubs who asked me to speak to them, and churches that invited me to speak or write poems for special services. And, of course, the many teachers who invited me to meet with their students, but especially Irmo High School, where I had the privilege and pleasure of extended work with creative writing students.

For collaborations I want to thank Jennifer Bartell, Evelyn Berry, Bee Boggs (best intern ever), Scott Chalupa, Ethan Focus, Josh English, Matthew Foley, Luke Hodges, Michael Krajewski, Monifa Lemons, Alejandro Garcia Lémos, the Spark Collective at USC (especially Sabrina Raber and Ben Haimann), Alexis Stratton, Barry Wheeler, and everyone at *Jasper*. For invaluable edits: Scott Chalupa, Nikky Finney, Ethan Fogus.

For support and opportunities related to this work, I also need to thank Bryan Borland at Sibling Rivalry Press, Caitlin Bright at Tapp's Arts Center, Michael Broder at Indolent Books, City of Columbia Parks and Recreation, the Comet bus system and Midlands Regional Transit, Fred Delk and Stormwater Studios, Mona Elleithee at Irmo High School, Sewell Gelberd and Columbia Council for Internationals, Indie Grits, Michael McKeown at the Good Men Project, Riggs Partners Create-a-thon, Erin Shaw Street, Joelle Ryan-Cook and the Columbia Museum of Art, Robin Waites and Historic Columbia, and the local businesses that participated in our public arts projects by distributing poems on coffee sleeves, on restaurant menus, with pharmacy prescriptions, and poems about haircuts.

Finally, I want to thank the community of artists and supporters within which I find myself. I could not have done many of these projects, nor would I have enjoyed this position as much without them. Although I know that I will forget someone, I have to list a few additional names: Bohumila Augustinova, Al Black, Eileen Blyth, Annie Boiter-Jolley, Bonnie Boiter-Jolley, Betsy Breen, Tracie Broom, Darion Cavanaugh, Tim Conroy, Adam and Bekah Corbett, Kristine Hartvigsen, Terrance Henderson, Patrick Kelly, August Krickel, Marion McClean, Kyle Petersen, Glenis Redmond, Joyce Rose-Harris, Ivan Segura, Barbara Thomson, Kendal Turner, Judy Turnipseed, Jason and Katy Watkins,

As I finish drafting these words a few days after Thanksgiving 2022, my heart is filled with such joy and love for Columbia's vibrant, resilient, brilliant, collaborative, and supportive arts community. I am so lucky that I landed here.

About the Author

Ed Madden served as the poet laureate for the City of Columbia for two terms, 2015-2022. He was the first city poet laureate in the state of South Carolina. He is the author of five other books of poetry, most recently *A pooka in Arkansas* (2023), which was selected for the 2022 Hilary Tham Capital Collection. Madden is a professor of English and former director of the Women's and Gender Studies Program at the University of South Carolina. He has also served as the literary arts editor for *Jasper* magazine. He is a 2019 recipient of an Academy of American Poets Laureate Fellowship, as well as artist residencies at the Hambidge Center in Georgia and the Instituto Sacatar in Itaparica, Brazil. In 2022, he received a South Carolina Governor's Award for the Arts.

www.ingramcontent.com/pod-product-compliance
Lightning Source LLC
Chambersburg PA
CBHW041129110526
44592CB00020B/2733